# THE 5 COMPONENTS OF LOVE

This book is dedicated to my mother. I dedicate this to her because I have witnessed her pain and anguish for many years and upon becoming aware of this reality, I've since wished you would know what I know. With this information, I truly believe she could change her life and her overall reality.

Princella Clark-Carr
The 5 Components of Love

Self-published
myvioletvisions@outlook.com

# TABLE OF CONTENTS

PREFACE

CHAPTER 1: The Journey to the Discovery of love

CHAPTER 2: Seek First Understanding

CHAPTER 3: Where Is Your Compassion?

CHAPTER 4: The Sacrificial Lamb

CHAPTER 5: Ensure Survival

CHAPTER 6: The Ultimate Sacrifice

**CHAPTER 7: There is no greater love than Self Love**

**CHAPTER 8: Possession**

**CHAPTER 9: Forgiveness**

## *PREFACE*

In November 2014, a young, aspiring model found herself in the throes of a distressing situation. The attractive mother of an eight-year-old son was entangled in a volatile relationship and wanted nothing more than to break the hold her emotionally unstable ex-lover had on her life. She never imagined she would end up here. Prior to their break-up, they were everyone's "couples goals"; a social media dream team. Their daily Facebook statuses consisted mainly of affirmations of their love for one another. The timeline was a collage of romantic, joyful pictures taken at various events; a collection of tender images set against backdrops of exciting cities that told a story of (what seemed like) a happy couple deeply in love.

And then, it all changed. When they parted ways, this once doting Prince Charming turned into a menacing cyber stalker. He harassed her mercilessly, showing up at her apartment and her job at all hours. He even set small fires in front of her home. He took to social media once again, this time to threaten her and post disturbing status updates that suggested he suffered from serious emotional instability. Most of their friends and family barely noticed the haunting messages. But she took note. She often asked herself, “What could have possibly happened to cause such a troubling change in his behavior?”

This is an all too familiar scenario. Romantic breakups are rarely (if ever) easy. Many people experience a myriad of emotions ranging from sadness to anger after splitting up. These feelings are normal, depending on who you talk to. Some may argue it is best to control the reactions; repress them; if possible, bury them. However, the most dangerous and detrimental thing any person can do is withhold emotion. This form of avoidance can severely affect the subconscious mind as it does battle with suppressed moods yearning for freedom. I've encountered people who not only believe emotions such as anger should be curbed, they are also convinced that love hurts, especially those who grew up on fairytales like Rapunzel, Sleeping Beauty, Cinderella, Snow White and Beauty and the Beast. They sincerely never envisioned love as something painful.

Anecdotal evidence shows that the negative feelings previously mentioned can be a by-product of love. What's more, those negative feelings can shift into negative actions. A basic understanding of the human psyche shows that emotion (complex states of feelings that result in physical and psychological changes) influence thought and behavior. Mary Lamia, a clinical psychologist and psychoanalyst writes: "A great deal of our decisions are informed by emotional responses because emotions are designed to appraise and summarize an experience and inform action". [1] In this book, I will explore the intensity of these powerful forces as it relates to love. I've seen first hand how potent the trajectory between love and the physiological reactions it elicits can be.

One evening in December of 2014 I came home, got comfortable, and began scrolling through my Facebook timeline. I take great pleasure in catching up on the latest news about my family and friends.

---

[1] Lamia, M (2010). Like It or Not Emotions Will Drive the Decisions You Make Today. Psychology Today. Retrieved from https://www.psychologytoday.com/us/blog/intense-emotions-and-strong-feelings/201012/it-or-not-emotions-will-drive-the-decisions-you

As I thumbed through current events I came

across a News 12 post from Shreveport, Louisiana. My heart jumped. The headline read, “Shreveport Woman Stabbed to Death”. The subtext: “Denied three restraining orders against ex-boyfriend.” Right there under the caption, a photo of a very familiar face. I recognized him as my old associate and military colleague. It turns out, one night he sat in the parking lot of his former girlfriend’s job, waited until about 4:00 a.m. for the woman to clock out, followed her home, ambushed her and slit her throat.

My mind was racing. I asked myself, what could possibly provoke such a tragedy? What fueled this fatal attraction? I began analyzing the events I just read about even further, posing questions I had often thought about, but now was ready to discuss. He killed this woman. Is this true love? Is love truly an emotion? If so, how can love, so sought after and enduring, be an emotion when emotions, by their very nature, are unstable? Think about it. Emotions can change from second to second, minute to minute and hour to hour. Therefore, if love is an emotion (as people perceive it to be) it stands to reason that a person can literally love someone today and hate them tomorrow. Is love-real love-that temperamental?

Many cases, like the one I just described between my associate and his ex-girlfriend, have a common theme: If I can't have you, no one else will". This particular tragedy ended with a slashed throat. Others end in gunshot wounds or vehicular homicide.

I recall watching a Facebook live video (sometime in 2017), where a man admitted to just murdering his ex-wife. During his wild rant, he kept proclaiming how much he loved her, yet he was confessing that he shot her in cold blood. As the story unfolded we learned the man had not actually killed his ex-wife. Instead, he had shot his son who tried to shield his mom and took a bullet meant for her. I was astounded to hear how many people, believe it or not, attributed the murderous actions of the crazed ex-husband to love. They reasoned, "He was hurt because he loved her and some men can't handle the loss of love". Social media is littered with similar comments. And I always counter the rationale by asking, "How can something that is supposed to be so positive be attributed to such negativity"?

After pondering long and hard about why people think this way, I came to the realization that many people do not understand the meaning of love. Why? Because lessons that have not been learned cannot be taught. Oftentimes, people are left to their own devices when it comes to figuring love out. They associate the experiences that dominate their reality with the overpowering feelings they display. However, making that connection does not require analysis. It's as easy as saying, "If 'A' happened and then 'B' happened, there must be some common link.

If you want to learn what love is, prepare to engage in deep thought and reflection. Without this introspection, understanding is lost and you are left with the belief that love is nothing more than just an emotion. Nevertheless, as previously stated, love is consistent and does not possess the unstable characteristics of emotion. I describe instability as bipolar, a "Dr. Jekyll and Mr. Hyde" state of being; a "thin line between love and hate". In my estimation, one can never hate something or someone he or she truly loves.

Ever since the dawn of human consciousness, great philosophers including Plato, Socrates, and Aristotle have questioned what love is. To this day, there is no real clear cut explanation from a layman's perspective.

In this book, I will outline the *Five Components of Love*. I have come to understand that love is not one thing, but a collection of five mechanisms. Love is a whole concept. The sum of all five factors must come together to constitute that whole, that love. I will give some examples of what love is and what it is not. Each will be tangible and practical. I will distinguish the differences between love and emotional attachments for a better understanding. It is with wisdom that I have gained from traumatic life experiences that have given me what I believe in and with a high-level insight on a simple, yet complex concept such as love.

While reading this book, you may notice that many of the concepts are repetitive. That is by design. It is written in a way intended to increase the probability you will grasp the concepts herein and train your subconscious to retain the main points. I truly believe with practical explanation and clarity (void of superstition and accepted dogma of what love is purported to be) readers will have more control over their lives, avoid situations that may do irreparable harm to their being and use this information to heal from previous damage.

I truly hope that, like me, you will be able to find value in this information.

# CHAPTER 1

# THE JOURNEY TO THE DISCOVERY OF LOVE

# CHAPTER 1

# THE JOURNEY TO THE DISCOVERY OF LOVE

The story that frames my entrance into the world will forever serve as a prologue to my desire to understand (and explain) the meaning of love.

As far as my mother was concerned, I was both her savior and her burden. Her ambiguity stemmed from a past littered with painful memories of abuse and disregard, often at the hands of her mother, my grandmother. Against a backdrop of hopelessness, on January 21, 1986 (a numbingly cold Tuesday) I,

Princella Clark, was born to a woman who struggled to earn recognition and love from her immediate family. And thus, my journey began. My mother, I was told, appeared happy at first. After all, she had just given life. “Joy to the world,” she whispered to no one in particular, as she held me in her arms for the very first time. "Someone who will finally love and cherish me," she informed the doctors and nurses as they busily carried on with the work of testing my vitals and post-delivery condition to make sure I was healthy. Her delight belied her true feelings. She was miserable, and the feigned attempt at contentment merely mask the fact that my mother suffered from severe emotional neglect and abandonment issues. Just the thought that she “finally” had someone to love raised a red flag. Why did she not feel loved before? When I was old enough to understand, my mother told me that she believed having a baby would complete her; ultimately, provide the affection she had never experienced.

As a child, I saw my mother cry far too often. Tears would stream down her face until her cheeks were soaked and stained with mascara. I was too young to understand how I felt about seeing my mother in this state, but thinking back, if I had to put it into words, I would say I pitied her. She would sit motionless for hours, her face virtually expressionless. It was evident that she was hurting inside, her sadness a silent, helpless cry for help. When I looked into her eyes, the pain I saw was gut-wrenching.

There were also outward signs my mother was suffering. She would write poems about committing suicide. She may have eventually taken her life were it not for her two small children. You could say, we saved her life, but ironically, to her, it was not a life worth salvaging. What happened to the love she thought she'd feel when her babies were born? Why was there still a gaping void in her heart, her soul?

It wasn't hard to figure out why my mother was so sad. One had only to observe how she interacted with her mother and sisters to understand why she was unfulfilled. They completely ostracized my mother. The people she longed to be close to (that she should have been close to) pushed her away. Let me put the dynamic in some perspective: My family is akin to a social club. There are the cool relatives who everyone spends time with. Then, there are the misfits who no one wants to be around. It's an unfortunate reality, exacerbated by the fact my grandmother pitted her children against each other by designating her favorites. This bias caused a rift among the siblings, a breach few of them knew how to deal with much less repair. My mother bore the brunt of my grandmother's indifference. She was often made to feel less attractive than her sisters, and nothing could convince them otherwise — not even a physical attack. Her sister's husband raped my mother.

She called to tell my grandmother who said her allegation could not possibly be true. After all, how could anyone be remotely attracted to someone as ugly as my mother? "Attracted to"? The lack of sympathy was beyond the pale however it was par for the course, another reason my mother was miserable.

Even when she tried to associate with her family, they made it clear she was persona non grata. They treated her like the "black sheep," even around the holidays; especially during the holidays. And it was not for her lack of effort. To prepare for Christmas and Thanksgiving, my mother would stay up all night cooking food for the family get-together. We had a lot of relatives; eight aunts and uncles, their children, and close family and friends. The Clark residence was bursting at the seams during the holidays. That said, her contribution should have been welcome. Not to mention, my mother was no slouch in the kitchen. Her culinary skills were top-notch, and many can attest to that. My grandmother was neither impressed nor grateful. She made sure no one else but my brother and I touched my mother's food while the rest of the family dined on my grandmother's fare. My mother had to go back home, with most of the food she had spent so much time lovingly preparing. To see her children marginalized and shunned destroyed her.

The damage her mother inflicted ran deep.

My brother and I did not escape our grandmother's wrath. She would refuse to feed us, even when she fed her other grandchildren. We'd watch her fix a big pot of rice and beans only to tell us there was not enough to go around. Meanwhile, everyone but my brother and

I received generous portions. She even saved dinner plates for my aunts, who would swing by after work to pick up their children. Some days we were given a choice; eat the days-old leftovers or they would be fed to the dog or thrown away. We literally played second fiddle to a household pet.

The pattern of abuse didn't stop at social gatherings. My family managed to make a planned road trip from Shreveport to Florida a master class in how to humiliate the grandchildren. My grandfather was supposed to rent a 16-passenger van for the 11-hour excursion.

My grandmother convinced him to rent a smaller model. The plan, intentional and mean-spirited, was devised to slight my brother and me; if there was not enough room in the vehicle, we could not go. And it worked. The whole family boarded the van and drove off, leaving us (two children, under the age of 10) standing outside until my mother got home from work around 9 pm. My mother was devastated; her greatest source of anxiety underscored: she now believed in no uncertain terms that neither she nor her children were loved by her family, for reasons none of us could comprehend.

As with most stories worth telling, context is everything. There has to be a basic understanding of how the journey began and what detours, obstacles, and rites of passage led to the eventual destination. As I lay the history of family bare, some may wonder why I choose to share the details of my upbringing. Because there has to be a foundation before I can begin building the structure, that being an understanding of how we mold our concepts of love.

My mother began to direct her pain at others. I seemed to be the preferred target of her ire. Me, her firstborn child, the one who was once her joy to the world, now a nuisance. Why?

These are the questions you ask when you do not fully recognize what love is. All you know, for the most part, is that you do not feel it. That is probably the main reason people buy into the notion that love is an emotion. They are analyzing their sentiments based on their interaction with other people. Love gets lost in the give and take and the back and forth; the noise of behavior mutes the meaning.

As for my interactions with my mother, I could not figure out why she mistreated me.

I am a very multi-talented individual. I can write, sing, draw and dance. I am an outstanding communicator. If a child is this smart and gifted, you would think her parent would be bursting with pride, overflowing with happiness. Not in my case. My mother was downright cruel. She's done everything from wishing I would go to school and be gunned down in a Columbine-like shooting so she could collect insurance money, to destroying a binder-full of cartoon artwork I poured my heart and soul into creating, ripping each drawing, page-by-page right in front of me to prolong the torture. The latter occurred when I was 10-years old. There is an adage that says, "hurt people, hurt people." That is definitely true. Her actions broke my heart.

She soon graduated to emotional and physical abuse. She's pulled handfuls of hair out my head, kicked me, thrown me to the ground, stomping my body until I was battered and bruised. By then, I was 13-years-old.

Ironically, one of the few times she showed compassion (and shed a tear on my behalf) was the day she thought I had gone missing. I had attended an after-school event as a member of the Fellowship of Christian Athletes Club. I'd told her I was staying after school, but she must have forgotten (or wasn't listening when shared the information). When I did not get off the school bus that afternoon, she assumed the absolute worst. She sobbed and fretted. When she realized I had not been kidnapped (or murdered), she showered me with "I love you's." You would have thought it was the end of days!

I was confused. Why the tears? The declaration of love? This reaction defied logic. How do you love someone you destroy emotionally? How do you love someone you castigate, psychologically dismantle, physically abuse? Nevertheless, I basked in the rare show of affection, however short-lived.

The emotional and physical abuse continued until I left her home.

On January 21, 2004, my 18th birthday, I joined the Armed Forces. I thought of it as a safety net and reasoned it was the only way I could transition to being on my own even if I was not thoroughly prepared. My mother tried everything in her power to discourage me. I needed a license, but she refused to teach me how to drive. She wouldn't hand over my birth certificate, high school diploma, and identification cards. Her mission was to make sure I failed at everything I attempted. I was lost. I wanted to function on my own yet had no idea where to start.

Her behavior was not a reflection of love.

The military became a way out; a means to escape the cruelty. I had had enough. I was less concerned about getting killed in war than I was about dying in the streets of my own country or at the hands of my mother. I left for basic training in May of 2004, four days after my high school graduation day. I learned basic skills that built my confidence. I wasn't wholly independent, but I was able to function autonomously. I realized too late that I made one mistake that I would soon regret. I joined the National Guard instead of enlisting for active duty. The former would give me an opportunity to attend college. The latter ensured I would never have to return home. It was bad judgment on my part and I paid the price. When I did go back home, nothing changed. I was still committed to pursuing higher education. I almost succeeded. Almost. The day I planned to leave Shreveport for school, my mother locked all of my bags somewhere inside the house, and I had no way to retrieve them. I never made it to school.

I was thrown out of her house shortly afterward and remained homeless for a time. I was nomadic, trekking from one person's residence to another's, trying to find a place to rest my head and find my way. My grandmother turned me away, wishing me well as she slammed the door to her two-story, five bedroom home in my face. I lived with one family that had a 14-year old child with little regard for anything around him. He set the house on fire. I escaped (barely) with second-degree burns on my leg. My next address was the home of a family friend whose intentions were, shall we say, were a bit too "friendly." Since I did not want that kind of relationship, I had to find somewhere else to stay. All I could think during this time is, this must be what it feels like to be unloved.

My last stop, the home of a high school friend. She let me stay with her for a while. I got a job at the Burger King near her house. It was there I met my very first boyfriend, and the first time (I believed) I would finally know love. Oh boy, was I wrong.

The relationship was fraught with emotional trauma, and I was debilitatingly insecure. It was doomed from the start. My boyfriend was a terrific guy; smart, attractive and charming. Since I believed I was not much to look at, I was shocked that a guy of his caliber wanted to date me. It was great while it lasted. We lived together, worked together and attended school together. One might argue we spent far too much time with each other. It worked until it didn't. My low self-esteem began to weigh on our relationship. I was angry, volatile, unreasonable, irritable. One night, I noticed he had spoiled a picture I drew for him. I lost it. It took me back to the time my mother ripped up my drawings. I was traumatized by her actions. He had no idea why I was so angry, but how could he have known?

The slightest thing would send me into a rage. It did not help that my self-esteem was so low growing up; I felt being born a girl, was a curse. I hated being a girl. Don't get me wrong; I was never sexually attracted to women. I just resented being one. I wasn't raised to embrace my femininity. Instead, I was conditioned to loathe it. One day, he was playing “The Whisper Song” by the Ying Yang twins. The lyrics “Hey bitch, wait till you see my dick," struck a nerve. The words were so degrading. I felt they somehow were a reflection of me! I snatched the CD out of the player and threw it out the window. He stood there, dumbfounded. These instances of unexplained anger finally took their toll. He eventually began cheating on me, and we broke up.

I moved in with another high school friend. While living with her, the light bulb finally went off. Obviously, I didn't know what love was. My failed relationship didn't provide answers. I would ruminate on the cliché, "You can't love someone else until you love yourself first," but I was still struggling to learn how to love (myself or anyone else for that matter). I needed to find the answer, or I would either fall into a deep depression and destroy everything in my life and eventually kill myself, or I would discover the inspiration I needed to start healing. It was during this moment of clarity that my journey of self-discovery began.

The truth is, only love has the power to heal.

I began to meditate on this concept for a long, long time. It raised more questions: "What is love?" "How do you do it?" "Is love tangible or intangible?" "Is it an emotion or is it an action." The one thing I knew for sure is, if you ask the brain a question, it is designed to find a perfect answer for you. Still, no one has genuinely answered this burning question; at least not without injecting some superficial concept into the mix or limiting the idea to pure (uncompromising) logic.

When I was seven years old, I was a devoted Christian. I read the biblical story of Solomon, which told the tale of how God gave him the option to have anything he wanted. He asked for wisdom. I was inspired. I too prayed for wisdom. Be very careful what you ask for because you might get it.

This journey toward knowing what love is was long and painful. To find the answer, I had to endure two physically abusive relationships, financial ruin, living on the streets in a city of seven million people that was unfamiliar to me, and a relationship that drained me to the point of emptiness and frustration. Answers did not come until 2016. It finally clicked. I was utterly divided between my emotions and my logic. I realized: Love is not an emotion. It is an umbrella built upon five components that never change. They are stable and consistent; unwavering.

I discovered that love, unlike emotions, is steady and firm. The journey had just begun.

# CHAPTER 2

# SEEK FIRST UNDERSTANDING

## Chapter 2

## SEEK FIRST UNDERSTANDING

*"Understanding comes through communication and through understanding we find the way to peace." ~John Locke~*

People who know me will likely tell you that I am the least religious person they know. I am an independent thinker and do not subscribe to any religious doctrine or believe in a "savior," even though I was raised a Christian. The reasons I choose not to endorse any hard and fast dogmas are personal, and I will not expound upon them in this book. However, the fact bears mentioning because it will help readers understand my stream of consciousness.

I am also what some call a millennial. With that designation comes a general characterization: the tendency to rebel against the old way of doing things. I definitely do not follow the status quo. I do believe there is truth in the elements (water, earth, air, fire) and even in many books (such as the bible), convictions which help us understand our reality and navigate our everyday world. I am also sure that many religious people do not study the parables in the Bible to comprehend their reality. My feeling is the faithful use the bible to gain a superficial awareness of God. The Bible is replete with wisdom and people would probably use it more to their advantage if they studied the tenets through a lens of simplicity.

Arguably the most powerful scripture in the Bible is, "For God so loved the world, he gave his only begotten son, that whosoever believes in him shall not perish but have everlasting life." This verse from John 3:16 sums up love and its five components. I will explain further later in the chapter.

We all lead busy lives. People are racing through their days and taking little time to interact with one another. We are socially detached, self-absorbed and lack personal human contact. Folks have become completely disconnected from reality. Dale Carnegie wrote in his book, *How to Win Friends and Influence People*, "Remember that a person's name is to that person the sweetest and most important sound in any language." Mr. Carnegie is spot on! We have lost sight of deferential recognition. Pay attention to people when they converse; you will find the term used most frequently is "I." It's as if they do not acknowledge the person they are speaking to. People are so caught up in their world; they do not listen to nor do they consider anyone or anything outside their interests. The tendency is prevalent in our fast-paced society.

There was a time, a person or family would move into a new neighborhood, and everyone would visit and greet the newcomers, perhaps bring a welcome gift. These days, folks don't even say hello to their neighbors when they pass them on the street. This lack of communication affirms that the majority of people in this world do not know love. You cannot love what you do not understand, and there can be no understanding without communication. It's a missing link.

People get carried away with using words they don’t comprehend. There is no sound grasp of phrases and terms; what should be simple dialogue becomes verbiage. Such obscurity renders words meaningless. Let’s take a moment to define the term “understand." According to Google Dictionary, it means, "To perceive the intended meaning of/be sympathetically or knowledgeably aware of the character or nature of.” This phrase illustrates why understanding is the first principal component of love.

"To be sympathetically or knowledgeably aware of the character or nature of" someone or something, a person must care enough to communicate. For example, if you say you love music, its appeal will arouse a burning desire within that will encourage you to learn everything you can about music. You will listen to lyrics, study songs, replay tracks; you will let the music permeate the deepest recesses of your mind until it consumes you. Many people mistakenly believe communication means two people, or several individuals *speaking*. However, the real art of communication is *listening*. To hear what someone is saying one must dispel egos, pay attention and respect their presence and recognize their importance. One of the most important forms of this exercise is *active listening*. Active listening is a communication technique widely used in counseling, certain forms of training, and conflict resolution. It requires the listener to concentrate, understand, respond and remember what is being said. Active listening requires focus. If a person is reluctant to listen to you, that means they are not willing to get to know more about your character. They are not interested in being sympathetic and not inclined to appreciate the unique details that make you who you are. Moreover, you can't love someone unless you love yourself first. You cannot become knowledgeable and sympathetic to someone else when you are not knowledgeable and sympathetic to yourself. The concept I just described is the root of the five components of love. The theory, as I have already stated, begins with understanding.

Unresolved personal issues make it very difficult to care about somebody else's problems. A person fighting their demons is limited in his or her capacity to empathize with another person's troubles. In that way, they are self-centered. These people have a hard enough time coping with their difficulties and do their best to avoid dealing with their struggles. They are concerned that speaking with others leaves them vulnerable. What if something that is said triggers an unwanted memory or forces them to look in a mirror and face the fact they are flawed. On the opposite end of the spectrum, you have those who ignore their own needs (because they do not value themselves) to cater to others. The trouble with taking that path is, the people they assist drain them of the energy they should be using to heal themselves. No one who loves themselves would engage in this form of self-sabotage. "You can't love someone without loving yourself first."

Let's reflect on John 3:16. From this point forward, we will use the viewpoints we've been focusing on in the place of love.

We've acknowledged the importance of the first verse, "For God so loved the world." God was knowledgeably aware of the nature of humanity's suffering and issues. He listened to the cries of the people; he was focused and paid a great deal of attention to humankind. Humans are imperfect creatures. They are a product of their environment and their past experiences. Every person's brain is wired differently and responds to external stimuli in unique ways. Specific words can trigger different responses depending on who hears them. For example, the word submissive.

When used in the context of a woman being *submissive to her husband*, the term will provoke varying reactions. Women who have had a negative experience with controlling men or were physically or emotionally abused hear the word and their mind will swell with negative emotions and images. Women who have had favorable experiences with men who treated them with respect and care will not be as affected by the word. It won't conjure up painful experiences because they associate positive feelings and a happy mindset with their relationship with men. Triggers generated by the spoken word, form as early as childhood. Past experiences further add to the buildup of a person's core character traits up until the age of 25, when the frontal lobe is completely developed.

When a person tells you they love you, they realize that the world does not revolve around them. They choose to be part of your world, your reality. Remember, you cannot do this for someone else if you haven't done it for yourself first. When a person does not do this for themselves, and instead focuses on the needs of others, they begin feeling unfulfilled, neglected. They are seeking validation from the other party in the hopes that person will satisfy the void they can't fill in themselves. Those who are not aware of their character find themselves in situations that are not conducive to their growth. They unwittingly do even more harm to their self-esteem.

My next example is controversial and may be uncomfortable for many people, but it's effective. Race relations is one of the most sensitive topics in today's society. The Black Lives Matter movement emerged in the wake of

Florida teen Trayvon Martin's murder. The unarmed teenager was gunned down by a neighborhood watchman, George Zimmerman, while walking home from the store. The subsequent BLM movement upset a lot of people. And they expressed their anger. I've heard many Caucasian people say they love everyone including black people. Still, anytime black people express legitimate concerns about race, pain, and anguish, these same Caucasians would rather silence them than hear them out. *A person cannot love you if they do not understand you*. A person cannot understand you if they are unwilling to listen to you. Many of these Caucasian individuals have not dealt with feelings and emotions having to do with race. Therefore, it is difficult for them to listen to a black person because they are unfamiliar and uncomfortable with their plight. The words black people, slavery, racism, etc. put them on edge. Many shut down emotionally and become defensive because their world consumes them and blinded by personal feelings. They align themselves (because of their skin color) with the perpetrators of these atrocities. They cannot disassociate from their ancestors. To assuage their guilty consciences, they silence black people to avoid awkward triggers. As long as people (of any race) remain self-centered and self-absorbed, there will never be peace or cohesion amongst human beings.

People often identify entertainment as a unifying force, but the unfortunate reality is, that is not the case. Entertainment distracts people from reality. Entertainment is a temporary event. When the event is over, reality sets back in. The distraction is gone. You must now listen and try to understand people outside this common interest. If you do not know how to do either with the opposite race, there will never be unity or cohesion. There will never be love across racial lines. One of my favorite quotes is, “Seek first to understand, then to be understood.”

There is an independent hip hop artist (Joyner Lucas) who wrote a song titled “I’m not racist." The lyrics tell the story of a white man and a black man conversing and listening to each other’s points of view. This kind of interaction is necessary to achieve healing and to make progress in race relations. We must listen and understand, or there will be no love, even if one says they love another race or all people. Lack of understanding gave rise to “All Lives Matter” which was created to counter BLM and drown out the feelings and concerns of black people who felt society devalued their worth.

The bible says, “Lean not on your understanding." This means people can only think about ideas based on limited knowledge of their own beliefs, feelings, and reality. To have a more in-depth understanding, you must tap into the culture and reality of others. The experiences of another race are unique to them. To relate, we need to understand the history from the lens of our truth. That point of view is limited if we do not open up the lines communication. It is not our job (nor is it possible) to tell people how to feel or force them to conform to what you want them to feel. You can only accept them as they are. Change comes from within. Feelings change when new knowledge and experiences shift perception.

Mr. Davis is a black man who, for the past 30 years, has spent time befriending Ku Klux Klan members. We all know KKK members harbor extreme beliefs against minorities, especially black people. The relationship between blacks and KKK members is not a healthy one. However, Mr. Davis convinced over 200 KKK members to throw away their robes. How did he accomplish this? Simple; through communication and established relationships. Remember, many people's negative feelings come from the fact that they have no intimate knowledge or connection with the people they have formulated opinions and beliefs about. Once a person has expressed a core belief, it shapes their perception, emotions, and feelings. Once Mr. Davis established a friendship with the KKK members who shed the robes, that gave rise to an experience which created a new understanding and ultimately transformed their feelings.

Understanding is the gateway to your emotions, the most necessary part of love. Emotion drives action. Humans are emotional creatures, and the decisions they make in life are based primarily on their emotions, not logic. This is why many children drop out of school or do not succeed in subjects like math. They lack the understanding to assimilate what is being taught. Lack of understanding fuels apathy. You don't care. Care means to *feel concern or interest; attach importance to something.* Many wealthy people who have always had wealth lack an understanding of those who are impoverished because they have not interacted with or understood the plight of impoverished people. They lack concern or interest in their suffering. There is no emotion on which to pin action, so all hope for love is lost.

True love can only come through understanding.

# CHAPTER 3

# WHERE IS YOUR COMPASSION?

# CHAPTER 3

*"If you want others to be happy, practice compassion, if you want to be happy, practice compassion" ~Dalai Lama~*

Every day, while walking down the street or driving my car, I see a homeless person or someone begging for money. I do not attach too much emotion to homelessness. My personal experience has numbed me to the condition. When I moved to Houston, I was penniless. I took up residence with my brother; however, that was short-lived. I was asked to leave and was summarily barred from the apartment complex when management learned I was not on the lease. I had nowhere to go, no money and an out of state license with several bench warrants attached. I slept on the streets of Houston but never stopped trying to make a better life for myself. Despite the circumstances, I never went to a shelter, and I did not beg for money. Those choices were among the few things about my situation I could control. It helped me preserve my dignity.

Eventually, I found a job in sales where I earned a commission. I got ready for work by showering at a local gym and never missed a day. I did everything in my power to avoid being homeless. That is why I find it so hard to understand why others, when faced with the same challenge, can't (or won't) take similar measures. I've talked to homeless people, interacted with them, and for the most part, a lot of people in that situation (that I met) do not seem interested in improving their lot in life. They are complacent. I have a friend who is always right on the verge of being on the streets. It's become some twisted mindset, a way of gaining sympathy. All these encounters have desensitized me to those who fail, for lack of trying, to find a permanent dwelling. I do not know why they are indigent and choose this predicament. I do not validate the decision. No doubt you will think me insensitive. However, I know I am not the only one who feels this way. I believe I am part of a majority.

I happened upon a video by ZDogg MD that was quite enlightening.[2] He was discussing the scientific functions of the brain that leads people to forget young children in automobiles to perish. He explored the science of human behavior

---

[2] Damania, Z (2018, July 10) A Fatal Distraction. Retrieved from https://www.facebook.com/watch/?v=10156383539702095

and the complexity of subconscious programming and studied the brain's tendency to switch to auto-pilot when a person is exhausted. He expounded on how the archaic wiring of the brain and the unreliable nature of memory can cause you to forget a child in a car. Even with this kind of scientific reasoning, many people were outraged. Comments like, "Sorry, no excuse at all no matter who you are. I don't care how much you work, how tired you are, nothing. I raise four children as a single mom, worked two jobs all the time around their schedules. You don't have to forget your kids unless you want to. Never forgive anyone who has done this" spoke volumes. This anonymous commenter and the over 700 people who approved of the sentiment online, refuse to understand the individual who made a fatal mistake. The reason? Most people believe the world revolves around them. They use their personal experiences and unique train of thought as a guide in their judgment of others. They do not consider that everyone is wired differently and personalities vary. There is an emotional disconnect which prevents them from accepting the information that would afford them the benefit of understanding.

On the contrary, another scientist addressing the issue I just wrote about commented: “You have to do something to break the brain’s autopilot. I’m a car seat tech and a flight paramedic. I always tell parents, if you’re scared of leaving your child in the car or if you are taking them somewhere out of your normal routine, take off a shoe and buckle it in the back seat next to your child. You might get out without your purse or phone or whatever else, but you will likely not forget your shoe when your foot hits the hot pavement. It's a low tech solution. I've been so sleep deprived before with some medications that I got home without remembering getting into my car. It can be terrifying. I've been in such an autopilot mode that something out of that normal routine gets completely missed, and my heart hurts for her and her family." Both comments above stem from the individual's personal experience and thought patterns. They judged the situation based on their informed reasoning.

Changing your way of thinking is hard. Actors and actresses are trained in the process, so imagine how difficult it is for the average person.

Understanding is the first step to love but what comes next? Emotion; the key ingredient to having the capacity to love. The specific emotion I am now referring to is compassion. Compassion is a sympathetic consciousness of others' distress together with a desire to alleviate it.[3] There can be no sympathy for circumstances you don't understand. Compassion is a critical component to love because it drives action.

[3] Retrieved from https://www.merriam-webster.com/dictionary/compassion

Compassion is the component that varies in percentages. The intensity of compassion will determine the extent of the action. There are people in this world who feel no empathy. Those are the folks who brutally murder innocent people with no remorse. There are those who are wholeheartedly compassionate and will give everything they have. Finally, there are those who fall somewhere in between.

Before writing this book, I was popular for my vlog talks on Facebook. That online platform is a great place to see what the masses are thinking. I have spent several hundred hours analyzing how people interact on different posts. I notice when people know nothing about another person's story, they are quick to hurl insults and destroy a person's self-esteem by attacking their physical appearance. If they learned the person they belittled was the victim of tragic circumstances, negative responses turned to positive messages. They begin to show sympathy.

In 2017, I followed the online story of an overweight girl. She posted photos of herself in her lovely prom dress for her family to see. The general public began making fun of her weight, and the pictures went viral. The mean-spirited antagonists chipped away at her self-confidence. It wasn't until she expressed how the smears hurt her so badly she did not attend her prom, that the name-calling transformed into words of encouragement.

Another famous example of this movement is the fiasco that flared up between popular comedian Monique and media services provider Netflix. Before people knew the whole story, they mocked her, ostracized and criticized her. There was little sympathy on her behalf.

However, once she began to explain what she was dealing with behind the scenes with the top brass and other influential industry insiders, the tide began to shift in her favor. More people sympathized with and supported Monique. They stopped short of boycotting Netflix. Budgets would not allow! People needed their affordable entertainment.

The point is, once people had the whole story, the mocking subsided, they considered her point of view, and the proliferation of emotion led to sympathy.

Much of my knowledge comes from reflection; analyzing my personal experiences and combining what I learn about myself with the external information I take in (from sources like science, math, and psychology). One of my most treasured experiences took place when I was a sales professional. I worked in sales and customer service for 15 years, in various roles. The experience taught me that stories sell. Customers buy stories. These stories are designed to build a rapport and connect with the client's emotional side. People would rather deal with the humanity in others. If you can tell a good story that caters to their emotion you increase your chances of making a sale.

When I worked in direct (better known as door-to-door sales), my team was pushing for a child sponsorship campaign. I was very good at the job. I mastered the most critical part of the endeavor: getting the potential sponsor to listen. Once you get their attention and the more heartfelt the story is, the more emotional the potential sponsor becomes, and closing the deal is easier. I excelled at the art of sales, and that helped me achieve a deeper understanding of human psychology and understand what motivates people to action.

If you pay close attention, you'll find everyone loves to talk, hypothesize, and sell fantasies, but very few people act. People love to be perceived as good or righteous but rarely exhibit those qualities or characteristics. They don't "sell" it. Ask yourself this: Is it possible to listen to everyone? Can you put your personal feelings about something aside and focus intently and objectively to everyone? Are you able to acquire knowledge about or be aware of the nature or characteristics of every single person you come in contact with? Is it possible to pity everyone's suffering (sincerely) without sacrificing objectivity? If you answered no to all these questions, you are not capable of loving everyone, contrary to what you may believe.

I do not subscribe to the notion that you can love everyone; it is not an attainable goal. Some people believe monks have reached the highest level of spirituality. This inference may or may not be true. However, the likelihood is higher because they understand that life is as it is, people are who they are and are where they are supposed to be at the time all this is intended. You cannot accept that reality if your sole purpose is to change others. You cannot have compassion or sympathy for someone who chooses a path of destruction and self-sabotage but refuses to be accountable for those actions. I discussed the idea of accountability and responsibility with an audience of several thousand. I informed them that willful ignorance is indeed a choice they have a right to make. However, they must be aware that they are 100 percent responsible for that decision and its consequences. I also informed them that once you become aware of the consequences, have weighed the pros and cons, the risk versus the reward, and you still decide to make a decision that is not in your best interest, I cannot sympathize with you, especially if you try to assign blame elsewhere.

So, do I have micro-compassion or macro-compassion? On a micro level, do I lack sympathy for a person when I am aware of the potential threat? Or, do I understand that some people must access specific experiences in their lives to relate: macro-compassion? It's like the person that knows lions are dangerous;

that the nature of a lion is to kill and hunt. Is it truly possible to have sympathy for a tourist who is devoured by a lion because he stepped out of his vehicle and taunted a wild animal? They were fully aware of the possibility existed. They knew the nature of the beast. How about the "daredevils" of our day? You know, the ones who go viral on social media by performing extreme activities like doing cartwheels on the edge of skyscrapers? Do we have compassion for the person who plummets 200 stories to his death when they were fully aware of the dangers of tempting fate at such heights?

Do we feel sorry they died, or pity their stupidity? I will wager, only those who witnessed the gruesome lion attack or the horrific fall will feel any compassion. Most others, will not. The majority of people have no clue what would entice anyone to provoke a wild lion or do flip head over heels on the edge of skyscrapers.

Understanding also leads to appreciation. Appreciation is defined as recognizing the “full worth of." Synonyms include “value”, “treasure”, “admire”, and “respect”. The earth is a beautiful place. However, every day we unwittingly destroy its beauty because we don’t understand the impact littering and burning fossil fuels has on our planet and its inhabitants. We can't fully recognize the full worth of planet earth because we do not understand the fundamentals of its ecosystem as a whole. Bees help provide some of the things we take for granted. If you are not aware of how bees contribute to your well-being, you don't realize why it is so important to protect them.

I've studied a wide range of subjects including cell biology, biochemistry organic chemistry, digital animation, sales, piano, audio engineering, project management, business and much more. The more information you assimilate, the more you appreciate things you would have overlooked. The more you learn, the more you realize how little you know.

To truly understand anything, you must commit to careful, deliberate thought and be willing to slow down and take it all in. Your thought process cannot be hurried, and external stimuli can not bombard your mind. You must think it through so intensely that you appreciate its value.

Once you've achieved the ability to be compassionate and appreciative, you are ready to act. Love must be attached to the action. Intentions mean very little — only tangible results and outcomes matter.

Action requires sacrifice.

# CHAPTER 4

# THE SACRIFICIAL LAMB

# CHAPTER 4
## The Sacrificial Lamb

*"Great achievement is usually born of great sacrifice and is never the result of selfishness."*

*~Napoleon Hill~*

One of the seven Army core values is selfless service. It means placing the welfare of the nation, the Army, and your subordinates before your own. Selfless service, the Army believes, leads to organizational teamwork and encompasses discipline, self-control, and faith in the system.

Accomplishing this goal is not easy. To place the needs of others before your own means sacrificing some of yourself so that others may benefit. In other words, you must surrender something of value for the sake of a person or thing you regard as more important or worthy.

I remember reading an article on Facebook about a young woman named Jessica Davis who adopted an ‘orphan’ from Uganda. The story (A two-part exclusive from CNN) described Jessica as someone with above average financial means and who always wanted to share her blessings and her Christian faith with those less fortunate. Jessica read somewhere that there are almost three million orphans in the East African country of Uganda. It became her mission to adopt a child from the region. She was sure her family could take a young boy or girl in a desperate situation, provide them with a loving home, and ultimately make something good happen in a difficult world.

The process was long and tedious. She used an international adoption agency. It took over a year to fill out paperwork and cycle through formalities before Jessica and her husband reached the point where they would meet the child.

Finally, they welcomed a six-year-old girl named Namata into their lives (about two years into the process). Questions arose soon after.

For some time after arriving at her new home, Namata tried to tell the Davis' that she was *not* an orphan. Jessica, thinking this was some adjustment mechanism or a way to cope with past abuse, ignored the child's claim. Jessica's ego and personal feelings prevented her from listening to what her newly adopted daughter was telling her. Before long, the truth was revealed. The agency the Davis' hired to help them legally adopt the little girl, was losing its accreditation after the State Department found evidence the organization failed to comply with industry standards.

Jessica finally listened to Amata, who confirmed she was removed from a loving family in Uganda under false pretenses. She learned the agency told Amata's birth mother (recently widowed) that they had found a wealthy American family who would sponsor the child, send her to school and provide her with basic needs. Amata, her mom was told, would return when she completed her studies. The organization even drew up false documents showing Amata's mother had signed away her parental rights. By the time she realized what was happening, the "sponsorship" agency had placed her daughter in an orphanage.

Jessica was devastated. Meanwhile, friends, family, even government officials were telling her to "keep her (Amata) if you want." She had to make a tough decision; keep Amata or sacrifice the desire to have the little girl in her family's life so she could " do the right thing". Jessica knew choosing the former would overwhelm her with guilt. She and her husband were not kidnappers. She chose not to give in to her ego.

The Davis' began a fervent search for the child's family and worked tirelessly to return Amata to her mother's loving arms. They eventually filed paperwork to have Amata's adoption vacated, and the Ugandan government gave parental rights back to her birth mother. Jessica turned the desire to adopt a child, the heartbreak of having to give her back into a call to action. She is now an activist against the practice of illegal international adoptions.

As I have pointed out several times throughout the book so far, understanding is necessary because it leads to compassion and sacrifice. Initially, based on her knowledge of how urgent the need was to adopt children from impoverished nations, she developed a heightened sense of compassion and sympathy for their suffering; so much so, it inspired her to sacrifice time, money, mental and emotional energy to adopt a child she thought was in desperate need. We are talking tens of thousands of dollars, over a year's worth of red tape and paperwork and countless hours of research about the adoption process (especially in Uganda), all to give a child a better life.

When the unfortunate scheme perpetrated by the adoption agency was uncovered, Jessica faced another battle: this one was with her ego.

Many people do not grasp the concept of the ego. I am not speaking from a metaphysical or philosophical point of view; rather, from a psychoanalytic perspective. The ego is one of the three divisions of the psyche that serves as the organized conscious mediator between the person and reality.

The inculcation of philosophical beliefs, likes, and dislikes defines personal identity. These principles help make up the individual self. Once a person subscribes to beliefs, they begin to attach emotions to these attitudes. Therefore, when you attack (or address) a person's beliefs, it is tantamount to a personal insult because his her individual identity is so intrinsically tied to the perceived reality. The emotions that arise from a perceived attack can be unnerving. For instance, if you are a super huge, die-hard, Dallas Cowboys fan who owns tons of Cowboys paraphernalia worth thousands of dollars, when someone disparages the team you are personally offended. It's as if *you* are the team. If anyone attacks the Cowboys brand, they attack you and, more than likely, you become defensive. Once you have taken this position, it is not easy to listen to the other person's perspective. You feel compelled to reject what you hear because your objective is to protect your identity. This conflict is the battle of the ego.

Jessica had to fight her ego's inclination to be a loving, good woman who wanted to do the right thing by adopting a child. Circumstances fueled feelings that were in direct opposition to that predisposition, so she blocked out Amata's persistent cries for help. When she set her feelings aside and listened to the child, she found understanding and consequently, renewed compassion for the child. Jessica sacrificed the ego's bias toward keeping the child. Compassion compelled her to reunite the young girl with her family. The sacrifice cost her additional time and money, but the painstaking effort to reverse the damage proved worthwhile.

All too often, people believe that love is possession. The end goal for these types of individuals is rooted in selfishness and emotional attachment. Remember, love is a by-product of sacrifice, and sometimes that means relinquishing your desires to allow someone a chance to fulfill their destiny. There is an old proverb that says, "If you love something, set it free.  If it comes back it's yours; if not, it wasn't meant to be."  The logic behind this adago is concrete and edifying.

To sum up this chapter: If a person does not understand the needs or the situations of others, they will not sympathize with their suffering. Therefore, they will be unwilling to give up something that they deem valuable or that they treasure to ease their anguish. When a person loves you, they consider you important enough and worthy enough to sacrifice their wants for your wellbeing. The bible states that "For God so loved the world he gave his only begotten son…" God understood the plight of humanity and had compassion for their suffering. Therefore He was willing to sacrifice something dear to Him: His son.

The bible subtly describes love in these five components.

The reason we sacrifice is to ensure something survives. This leads us to the next chapter.

# CHAPTER 5

CHAPTER 5

# ENSURE

# SURVIVAL

# CHAPTER 5

## Ensure Survival

*"Love and compassion are necessities, not luxuries. Without them, humanity cannot survive." ~Dalai Lama~*

This chapter focuses on survival. Before we begin, I want to turn your attention once again to John 3:16: "For God so loved the world He gave his only begotten son, that whosoever believe in Him shall not perish but have everlasting life." This scripture serves as a perfect conduit for my reasoning throughout the book.

Now, let's explore the word survive, which means to continue to live or exist, especially in spite of danger or hardship. Words and phrases that are similar include: to remain alive, live, pull through, to keep body and soul together.

The aforementioned biblical reference and the meaning of survival are not mutually exclusive. Both must be taken with one accord. Combined, they underscore the meaning of love. Simply put, God first understood the plight of humanity. He then had compassion for their suffering. He ultimately gave His only son to ensure that humanity would continue to exist, despite their pain.

Ultimately, when you truly love something or someone, you want to ensure that it lives on.

One of the advantages of surfing social media is, every so often you happen across stories you would not usually read if you were not connected to the internet. My social media algorithms are set in such a way controversial material trends on my timeline. One such story is that of a four-year-old murdered by her mother and her boyfriend. Before this tragedy, the child's father tried for a year to gain custody, but legal hurdles and trouble navigating the nebulous welfare system. According to the father, the courts did not act with any degree of urgency on his behalf. While he was busy fighting these battles, his daughter was murdered.

These stories are upsetting. They leave people saddened, distraught and disgruntled; wondering how children could meet such a tragic end, seemingly without consequence. Unfortunately, this will not be the last time we hear about a child murdered by their biological parent (or parents). It is easy to say you love children, but to show you mean it, you must make their survival a top priority; love without conditions.

The bible says, “my people suffer from the lack of knowledge.” Allow me to paraphrase-people are ignorant; uninformed about many issues. It’s been said that ignorance is bliss and what you do not know won’t hurt you. This thinking is misguided. Ignorance is a conduit to the very conditions people insist they would rather avoid. A father should never have to deal with the pain of losing his child under such unfortunate circumstances. However, there is a common thread between this story and others like it: ignorance. If people truly wanted to keep children safe, they would learn more about the nature of child abandonment, neglect, abuse, and what leads to the death of a child. This is not a popular opinion. When I share the point of view, it is usually met with swift backlash, mostly from critics who cannot see beyond their emotions. Remember, that inclination (letting emotions cloud judgment), precludes listening.

The behavioral patterns of humans and animals are similar. One thing that separates man from beast is the ability to reason. Psychology determines how all humans respond to the world around them. These days, people are responding without careful consideration of their circumstances. For instance, very few men and women get to know each other before they become romantically or sexually involved. They have children with mates that are practically strangers. Couples don't know anything about each other's childhood, past relationships, philosophies on the environment. When you enter a union blind to how a person's background make up their personality, you leave too much to chance. Availing yourself with knowledge of such things illustrates how your environment, where you live, how you live, effects the psyche of humans (and animals).

People who subscribe to a particular religion usually make decisions based on whether the person they are pursuing shares their beliefs. Religious doctrine supersedes observing a person's character, history, relationships with others, job stability, etc. There is no in-depth investigation into what makes the person tick. In the case of a religious person, they are satisfied just knowing a love interest attends church. It stops there. There is no further assessment.

Belief is the acceptance that a statement is true of something that exists. However, when we accept things as true without an acute assessment of all factors, we set ourselves up for failure.

It is interesting how this kind of unchallenged belief system is so prevalent among devout church-goers, yet they are the people who are typically mired in some scandal. People given to religiosity scrutinize secular behavior that they engage in. Religion teaches people not to judge a person by his or her actions. From a biblical perspective, this message is not only dangerous; it is rooted in fallacy. First, by its very definition judgment suggests evaluation. Judgment is defined as the ability to make considered decisions or come to sensible conclusions. The synonyms are discernment, acumen, sense, common sense, wisdom, wit, reason and *logic*. To consider is to think carefully about something before making a decision. To wit, in order to think, you must observe and analyze people and then form a sensible conclusion about them employing logic and reasoning.

Secondly, the bible tells us we have the right to judge others. Psalms 82:6

states, “I have said, ye are gods, and all of you are children of the Most High." Psalms 82:1-5 says “God standeth in the congregation of the mighty; he judgeth among the gods. How long will ye judge unjustly and show partiality to the wicked? Defend the poor and fatherless: do justice to the afflicted and needy, deliver the poor and needy: rid them out of the hand of the wicked. They know not; neither will they understand, they walk on in darkness: all the foundations of the earth are out of course." Therefore, religious people who turn to the bible for the Word should not preach about withholding judgment. If you do not judge, you cannot dole out justice for those you claim you love. You won't be able to help them when they suffer at the hands of the wicked. To know someone is evil, you must observe, analyze and come to sensible conclusions about said person. Without careful analysis, you can't shield those you love from evildoers. Any belief that hinders the critical thinking process is not a healthy conviction. It is self-destructive; it allows you to bask in the ignorance from which the bible says we will all suffer.

Another detrimental ideology is that stereotypes are wrong and prejudicial. However, this is not entirely true. Many stereotypes are rooted in truth and reality which is linked to the overall authenticity of probability. When you encounter a stereotype, you must accept the probability that the label might very well be accurate. Humans are products of their environment. All races, humans, and genders form stereotypes based on an inherent cultural foundation entrenched in the reality of the tradition. Life is made up of probabilities and percentages; there are few absolutes. No human being can say with certainty that something is not possible. It is more realistic to surmise an unwelcome outcome is not likely. Condoms are not 100 percent effective. They were not designed to eliminate the chances a woman will get pregnant. Instead, they decrease the chances. The more people are informed about the contributing factors which yield undesired results, the more control we will have in the outcome. I do not want to see a child slain. I do not want to see someone's heart get broken. We can't change what that father has endured. However, we can use his pain to learn and take actions to limit these incidents. The lessons can potentially save more children in the future. A pebble thrown in the ocean still affects the waves.

A successful Richmond, Virginia businessman with a wife and two children was murdered during a robbery attempt. He was married 16 years. He and his wife owned a vacation home in Lauderhill, Florida. He took a trip to the sunshine state alone and participated in extracurricular activities a married man had no business engaging in. He was flashing his material possessions and caught the attention of three young, attractive females. He took them back to his hotel room, unaware he was being set up. The women robbed, shot and killed him.

I conducted a live video discussion about this event, to get a sense of what people thought. Most argued that the decision to cheat on his wife did not devalue his love for her; however, I disagreed, considering my theories on "The Five Components of Love". When a man has a family, wife, and children, their welfare comes before his selfish desires.

Love requires selflessness and sacrifice. A man who truly loves his family wants nothing more than to preserve its survival (and his). He understands that his family depends on his guidance and will not place himself in unnecessary danger. This man was well aware that the world we live in is full of criminals; an underworld infested with pimps in that game who feed off individuals like this man. These schemes often end in the victim's death. Not to mention, you can't love someone without first loving yourself. If he was not worried about his welfare, he surely was not concerned about the well-being of his loved ones. Society is full of single men and women who lived dangerous lifestyles while dating yet changed their behavior when they got married and had children. They realize they needed to survive for the sake of their family. They set aside their personal interests.

As for the man I just wrote about; his children now have to grow up without a father because he was careless and selfish.

Many people foolishly claim that all love is different; that the love you have for your mother is different from the love you have for your wife, children, siblings or pet. This is false. All love is the same; very consistent. The only difference is the intimate expression of the love. Intimacy (or being closely acquainted; familiar, close) can be expressed by taking your mother out to her favorite restaurant for a special Mother's Day dinner or by surprising your child with a birthday party that features their favorite cartoon character, or by spending time with your dog at tho dog park. You might even treat your spouse to a romantic evening, complete with rose petals and a bubble bath. Each expression of love, unique, varied and specific, is designed to see the happiness in their eyes.

The five components apply to each act. If you love your mother, your spouse, your children or your pet, you will actively listen to them to learn about their character. You will have compassion for their suffering and appreciate them. You will give up things that are valuable to you (time, money, energy) to make sure they do not suffer. You will sacrifice to ensure that they survive. If you love your mother, you want to see her live on. If you love your spouse, you want to see him or her live on, if you love your children, you want to see them live on. If you love your dog, you want to see it live on. Each individual requires distinct sacrifices to make them feel special.

Animal lovers have risked a lot to save the lives of injured furry friends and ensure their survival. You can find many of these stories on the Facebook page, "The Dodo." I read about a kitten named Hank, rescued by a lady called Hannah Shaw (known as the "Kitten Lady"). She got a call from animal control about a kitten in a tissue box abandoned at Petco in a tissue box. She immediately decided to check it out. When she arrived, she noticed the kitten, a newborn, had a number of health problems. The kitten was infested with fleas and had a severe eye infection. She brought the kitten to her home, fed it, rid it of fleas. She nursed the kitten back to health, but then Hank suffered a setback. Hannah took her to the Veterinarian, who diagnosed Hank with feline panleukopenia. The Kitten Lady was devastated. She was determined to keep Hank alive even though odds were not in the kitten's favor. Statistics showed that over 90% of felines inflicted with this illness die. Hannah did her research and settled on a course of action to combat this illness. When the virus attacked, the Kitten Lady countered with treatment. She kept Hank hydrated and comfortable, took her temperature, monitored her energy level, tracked her fecal samples and kept meticulous notes documenting her care. The kitten survived.

To truly love something or someone, requires time, energy and the sacrifice of your ego.

That said, is it truly possible to love everyone and everything?

# CHAPTER 6

# THE ULTIMATE SACRIFICE

# CHAPTER 6

## The Ultimate Sacrifice

## Willingness to Die For

*"Our lives are not fully lived if we're not willing to die for those we love, for what we believe."*

*~Martin Luther King Jr.~*

Making the ultimate sacrifice by giving up your life for another.

The idea is difficult to fathom, especially for anyone who believes they are the center of the universe. There is no place more comfortable than the safe haven that is the mind of a man or woman who thinks solely about themselves. This concept is different from sacrifice because to lay down one's life for someone else is a choice; one you must be willing to make no matter what. If you are not prepared to do so, love does not exist. You may care about someone. You may even like someone. However, if you are not willing to surrender self-preservation for the sake of their survival, you do not love. Let's be clear; you do not have to be a martyr for love. Just be willing to make the offering if circumstances warrant.

Numerous examples underscore my theory. In the Bible, Jesus accepted the burden because Christ loved humanity as much as Father did. Jesus gave His life to save our collective souls. Denzel Washington delivered a striking performance in the movie "John Q," one that also embodies the ideology I am writing about in this chapter. Denzel plays John Quincy Archibald, a father whose son has a cardiac condition and who is in desperate need of a heart transplant. John Q. loved his son dearly. His deep understanding of his child's condition fueled compassion and sympathy. As a result, this father (driven by an instinctual need to save his son) sacrificed his time, his money and even risked his freedom to that end. He was relentless, so much so, he took extreme measures. He shut the hospital down and took doctors, nurses, and patients as hostages. He was going to ensure that his son had a fighting chance, by any means necessary. He no longer cared about his freedom nor did he consider the possibility he would go to jail. His ultimate goal was saving his son. The pressures of this now very public, very critical situation on the hospital's administration and staff galvanized a search for a donor match. When that proved unsuccessful, John Q decided, he must die so his son can live.

He was willing to kill himself. Moments before he pulled the trigger, they found a heart for his son. Moviegoers cheered the happy ending.

John Q is obviously a work of fiction; however several real-life stories mirror the movie's premise. There is a story out of Japan that has made the social media rounds over the past several years. Some say it is unsubstantiated, and others believe it to be true. I share it because just the thought of this occurring reinforces my theory. A deceased woman was found in the rubble after a massive earthquake struck in Japan. The corpse had seemingly been kneeling (possibly praying) before she perished. The team of rescuers after confirming she was indeed deceased had to move on; the search and rescue mission was still underway throughout the city. One member of the search team felt compelled to return to the site where they found the woman. He began digging again. Much to his astonishment, he discovered a baby, still alive, covered by a blanket. The infant's mother is thought to have sacrificed her own life to save her child. Rescuers reportedly discovered a cell phone near the mother’s body; a text message on the device reading: “If you can survive, you must remember that I love you.”

Whatever you may think about the Armed Forces, conventional wisdom holds that the men and women on the frontlines are fighting for the freedom and protection of the citizens of their country. People join the military for a variety of reasons. I want to focus on the ones who join they love their country and willingly risk their lives to preserve freedom; to possibly die for a cause they truly believe. They may not die in combat, but they are willing to do so.

My grandmother and grandfather were together for over 35 years. As far as I can remember, there was always some discord in the relationship, instigated (it seemed) mostly by my grandmother. My grandfather, a dvvtruck driver who was always on the road, bore the brunt of her ire. She was known for saying hateful things when argued. As a child, I always felt my grandfather loved my grandmother more than she loved him.

My uncle was quite a burden on my grandparents. He was in and out of prison and a chronic substance abuser who spent a lot of time in rehabilitation centers. I also believe he had a mental disorder (possibly schizophrenia, which runs on my grandmother's side of the family). My uncle was also subject to seizures. One day- in 2007 or 2008; I don't quite recall the exact year- my uncle was at my grandparent's house (one of the rare occasions he was not in jail). Doctors prescribed medication but did not believe he needed any treatment. Sadly, when he was off his meds, he would tell people he saw demons, evil, and wickedness. These hallucinations made it unsafe to have him around. I am not sure what sparked this particular episode, be he grabbed a knife, fully intending to attack my grandparents. My grandfather happened to be home and stepped in to shield her from a vicious attack. My uncle stabbed him in the head multiple times. This selflessness and courage, to me, confirmed what I always felt; my grandfather loved his wife more than she loved him.

Fortunately, my grandfather survived that assault and lived four more years, before succumbing to a heart attack. After his death, something happened that confirmed in my spirit what

I had always felt. I believe, without any doubt, my grandmother would have never risked her life to save her husband. I will take the reason I now know this for sure, to my grave.

History is replete with philosophies. Some we agree with, others we discount, refute or reject. Many of these beliefs are fostered by a person's love for a specific group of people. When you speak about Dr. Martin Luther King, Jr. or Malcolm X, one fact endures; both activists dedicated their lives to serving the people they believed in. They stood up for a cause they were devoted to, heart and mind, in defense of people affected by the reprehensible actions of others. Eventually, they made the ultimate sacrifice.

True love stems from a willingness to die for an individual or a group of people. There is no greater sacrifice than giving your life to prolong the life or existence of a person (or purpose) you claim to love sincerely.

# CHAPTER 7

# SELF LOVE

# CHAPTER 7

## Self-Love

*"The most beautiful people we have known are those who have known defeat, known suffering, known struggle, known loss and have found their way out of the depths. These persons have an appreciation, a sensitivity and an understanding of life that fills them with compassion, gentleness, and a deep loving concern. Beautiful people do not just happen." ~Elizabeth Kubler-Ross~*

One maxim that I have underscored throughout this book is, you cannot love someone without first loving yourself.

Society is filled with men and women who insist on beating themselves up as some sort of penance for making a few mistakes in life. There is an increasing population wandering through their daily routine, with a notable air of semi-contentment, but beneath the surface, they are ashamed of their mental and spiritual scars. Their shame is so profound that, in order to deal with its effects, they project; they assume the role of victim, blaming others for their lot in life. Some simply ignore the feelings altogether. Others frame their reality around the values and beliefs of others, or they look to overarching cultural philosophies to define themselves.

All this avoidance of one's authentic self fuels shame.

Psychological abuse often begins in the home. Parents who mistreat their children; abuse them mentally, verbally or physically. They kids carry the wounds from that mistreatment with them, and the pain is exacerbated when they encounter bullies or are exposed to images and themes in media that play on their insecurities.

The bottom line is, you can't hide from your shame. Life goes on, and eventually, someone, something, or a specific experience will remind you of the very reality you've been trying to avoid.

A person consumed by willful ignominy and who is running from a self-image they despise are loath to confront the person they are and often feel they don't even deserve to be happy. They are self-deprecating; convinced they are worthless. Their actions and words are designed to show everyone around them that they undervalue themselves. The internal discord is amplified when they try to live up to other people's expectations. When there is conflict within the self, people cannot genuinely be selfless. Individuals cannot sincerely hold the interests of others above their own because while doing for others they are always thinking about personal fulfilment and the things they feel are missing. Most of the time they merely want acceptance from others.

When I was a child, my father was not really around. His absence was understandable to a certain degree. He was in the Navy. He began his military career at 18 years old. He married my mother, and I was born shortly after, in 1986. Two years later, my brother came along. My parents remained married for seven years before legally separating in 1993. My father served 23 years in the military. My mother moved back home to Shreveport, Louisiana with my brother and me. Once they separated, we did not hear from my father much. When he was on military leave, he would come to Shreveport, but my brother and I were not on his list of priorities. He didn't spend any time with us, opting instead to visit friends and his brother. He had a severe drinking problem, so they would mainly meet up, and drink beer. A lot of it. It is safe to say he was most definitely an alcoholic. He was a drunk until the end of his military career, which did not end honorably. He left the service with nothing to show for his many years of active duty. We never knew why.

Fourteen years after a military career that spanned more than two decades, my father reconnected with my brother and me, albeit our interaction is limited. He's been sober since retiring from the military and works as a service technician for a major corporation. One might say, my father is a shining example of recovery and growth. But there is one big problem; he traded one addiction for another. My father is a workaholic. He has not missed a single day of work in over 14 years (at the time of writing). He foregoes vacations, goes into work on his days off, and is typically the first one in the office and the last to leave. When we do speak with him, his conversations are rote, and his phrases are monotonous and brief. Something is terribly wrong.

Based on his behavior, I presume he is chastened that bad choices cost him 23 years of his life. He is trying to offset disgrace by overcompensating. He is trying to make up for misused years by creating a new, more productive and respectable timeline at this major corporation. Since he no longer abuses alcohol to suppress painful memories that haunt him, he works to the point of exhaustion. If he has no energy, he will fall asleep; his escape from a reality he does not want to confront.

Interestingly enough, if you pay close attention to some of the things my father says, he is clearly struggling with feelings of deep regret. He is so hard himself; trapped in the mental prison of his dark past. I can see that he wants a relationship with his children, but ego and remorse are preventing him from moving on with his life. He does not understand that, although his past is part of who is, he does not have to despise himself because he made foolish decisions. He believes he is already dead inside and refuses to live. He is trying to account for time he cannot recover.

My father is only 55 years old. Many people have lived to be 100 years old. That said, it is entirely possible that if he takes care of himself and reduces his stress, he can live a long time. His life can be re-claimed and enjoyed. But he must stop clinging to the past. Sure, he missed out on his children growing up, but he has two grandchildren that would love nothing more than to have him in their lives. However, he will not be able to love them or anyone for that matter, until he loves himself first.

My father has not accepted that life is a journey and along the way, you will encounter your fair share of bumps and bruises. These experiences help expand your consciousness. Without this understanding, he may never appreciate the path he's been on and will likely keep resenting himself for taking that discouraging passage to his current state of despair. There is always collateral damage from this way of thinking. He projects the by-product of his negative thinking onto others, perhaps believing they will punish him too. His ego won't submit to the punitive responses of others, and therefore he shuts people out of his life as a defense mechanism. He's become an island. He does not treat himself with any compassion and is unaware that he is running from his past, right into a world of hurt. His ego is in over-drive, driving his fear of condemnation and rejection. He is numb to the wishes of his children and grandchildren.

We are hurt. We want a relationship with him, but my father refuses to put that longing above his insecurities. Love requires selflessness, which is unattainable if you are broken inside. Only someone who is whole and self-actualized can give of themselves to others with no regret and without expecting anything in return.

Life is a journey, not a destination. The sooner we learn this, the sooner we can be at peace with where we are in life. When we accept our journey, we can be more fulfilled when we travel along the path. There is no danger in giving other travelers on the same route directions. The only way you can do this is by being selfless.

# CHAPTER 8

# POSSESSION

# CHAPTER 8

# POSSESSION

*"If you love a flower, don't pick it up. Because if you pick it up it dies and it ceases to be what you love. So if you love a flower, let it be. Love is not about possession. Love is about appreciation."*

*~Osho~*

One of the things I consistently observe in human beings is, some believe they are completely beholden to another person. Whether they are aware of it or not, they display signs of emotional attachments rather than any form of love. This need for another person to be there for them, approve of them, to like and love them no matter what, is usually rooted in fear.

Elizabeth Kubler-Ross wrote in the book "Life Lessons: Two Experts on Death and Dying Teach Us About the Mysteries of Life and Living", *"There are only two emotions: love and fear. All positive emotions come from love, all negative emotions come from fear. From love flows happiness, contentment, peace, and joy. Fear usually gives way to anger, hate, anxiety and guilt. It's true that there are only two primary emotions, love and fear. But it's more accurate to say that there is only love or fear, for we cannot feel these two emotions together, at exactly the same time. They're opposites. If we're in fear, we are not in a place of love. When we're in a place of love we cannot be in a place of fear."*

After pondering this construct for years, I can say with assuredness that I agree with Kubler-Ross.

Emotional attachment stems from a lack of self-love. Those who find themselves emotionally attached dread the idea of not having enough or all of a person. They worry someone else will benefit from the gifts or advantages the object of their desire has to offer. They are convinced that they will be denied the energy the person provides, the validation that fills a void. This apprehension makes them possessive; they begin to smother, suffocate, and destroy the very person they claim they love and even keep them from expressing their actual personality. Many people in possessive relationships are not allowed to have friends, dreams or goals and they aren't allowed to enjoy themselves without someone keeping tabs on them.

I love the early music renderings of genres such as Rhythm and Blues (R&B) and Pop. The lyrical compositions had much more thought and meaning incorporated into the pieces than the songs of today. Michael Jackson's "She's Out of My Life" from his "Off the Wall" album held that love is not a possession; it is a feeling that should be expressed without hesitation or disruption. Think about your personal relationships with either your spouse, your ex-spouse or significant other or even your children? Do you even speak to your kids? Have they distanced themselves from you? If so, could the underlying reason be that they were never allowed to be their own person when you were around? I've found, many children grow up traumatized from being treated as property by their parents. Others grow up struggling to discover their identity while also trying to prove to their parents or the world that they are their own person.

The lyrics of the song "Numb" by the popular alternative metal band, Linkin' Park, describe the pain of being denied one's individuality; being pressured to be a person whose character is molded to someone's expectations. The song's writers, Chester Bennington and his longtime friend Chris Cornell, committed suicide months apart. I wonder if the message in these lyrics mirrored their reported lifelong battles with depression? If so, anyone who claimed they love either of these men should never have tried to quell their self-expression. That would only have contributed to their depression. When people feel as though they cannot express themselves and be who they are deep down inside, they feel like prisoners trapped in 24-hour lock down; restricted to solitary confinement. If you prevent someone from seeing the light of the day, they will eventually lose their mind.

I have similar experiences with my mother. She thinks she can dictate my life and tries to control what I think. My mother believes giving birth is a right of possession. At the same time, some people remain tethered to their parents so they can be absolved of guilt when their mom and dad pass away. They believe severing ties suggests they don't love their parents. This sense of obligation pressures them to keep toxic individuals around.

The reality is you must never compromise your emotional stability or your life will spiral downward. You do not have to hold on to something to call it love. Love in most cases means letting go and allowing people to continue on their journey without you. In these situations, it is ok to cut these bonds through forgiveness.

# CHAPTER 9

# FORGIVENESS

# Chapter 9

## Forgiveness

"There is no love without forgiveness and there is no forgiveness without love" ~Bryant H. McGill~

In January 2018, USA Today published an article about the murder of 39-year-old Suliman Ahmed Abdul-Mutakallim. Mutakallim was shot in the back of the head by 14-year old Javon Coulter during a robbery attempt on June 28, 2015, while walking home from a White Castle in South Cumminsville. He died the next day. The senseless murder rendered even more tragic when authorities discovered the victim had less than $60.00 in his pocket at the time of the shooting. The two teenagers charged in the man's death pleaded guilty to involuntary manslaughter and aggravated robbery. At a court hearing two years later, the mother of the slain victim did a remarkable thing; she hugged her son's killers, and embraced Javon's mother, ultimately forgiving her son's killers.

The adage, "You need to forgive so you can move on with your life," is a common, somewhat overused platitude, but it is still salient advice. One does not forgive for the sake of the other person;

one pardons an offender to free themselves. When you're angry and upset and feel both emotions deep within your core, it is tough to understand. It feels as if you're absolving the person who caused you pain and heartache of any responsibility. In most cases, the weight of these negative emotions triggers a downward spiral in a person's life, partly because many of us were never taught how to forgive.

It takes love to forgive. I've offered you the guideline; if you process through the five components of love genuinely, you can begin to forgive.

Reportedly, the mother of Suliman Abdul-Muttakalim, Rukiye Abdul-Mutakallim, wanted his assailants to know she could pardon the heinous act that took her son's life. This merciful act took a great deal of understanding on her part. I will hazard a bet, most people in this situation would be so overcome with emotion their egos would take over, making it impossible to have any consideration for the person behind the senseless murder of their son. But remember, *understanding* is the first component of love; without understanding, there is no love, and without love, there is no forgiveness. The road to forgiveness is not easy, because it requires a great deal of selflessness to step into someone else's shoes.

Ms. Abdul-Muttakalim was not only understanding, but she also pledged to do everything in her power to make Javon a better man. Odds are, many people would hold too much hatred toward their child's killer to even think about helping them change. They would likely want them to suffer as they do; misery loves company. Forgiveness eludes them, negativity wells up in their subconscious, and in time the person destroys themselves from the inside out.

The one thing people whose thoughts are rooted in reality must understand is, nothing is real. Your mind is a canvas upon which the world you see is painted every day. You are the architect of this world. The question is, how does a person begin seeing what lies beneath the surface? There is a technique called "reframing" that can help you explore creation more deeply. Reframing allows you to tell a story in a way that will enable you to be the victor instead of the victim. You do not have to lie; however, you must be able to flip the position or spin how you internalize events that have transpired.

A perfect metaphor to support this thinking is, "The cup is either half empty or half full." For example, you are 15 minutes late to work because everything that could have gone wrong has gone wrong. The night before, your power went out while you were asleep causing your phone to die, which disabled your alarm. Therefore, you woke up late, and while rushing spilled coffee on your pants (and have to change into another pair). That adds another five minutes to an already hectic morning. When you begin traveling to work, you get a flat tire. As these events unfold, you are consumed with anger. If you tell yourself, “When it rains it pours, bad things always happen to me, why can’t things go right?”, this frame of mind will only fuel your anger and cloud your thinking, which can cause further mishaps. If you adopt the reframing technique, you will diminish or eliminate the negativity, and stay in control.

Reframing fuels positive thinking like, “There must be a reason that things happened this way” or “Maybe there was a serious accident that I would have been involved in had these chains of events not ensued…", or "Everything happens for a reason." If you think about seemingly unfortunate circumstances in this manner and BELIEVE your optimistic reasoning, it will inevitably reduce the negative feelings that could invade your psyche. This thought process is real because many people who did not make it to work on September 11, 2001, likely faced similar inconveniences and were frantic and upset about being late until they saw the news. When the gravity of what they avoided set in, they were thankful for what they initially thought was a series of frustrating events.

Ms. Abdul-Muttakalim employs the reframing technique very well. She held that “His death was already ordained…” Instead of believing, "They took my child, he had so much to live for; I am nothing without my son, they are evil…". She trusted that a person’s time is accounted for and when it is up, it will end in a way that is predestined. She had faith in the notion that everything happens for a reason and we derive something from every life experience, even if it’s painful. By viewing reality through this lens, she was able to reduce and eliminate negative emotions such as anger and animosity toward her son's killers. I am not suggesting she will not be anguished; however, her angst will subside over time. After the sentencing, she said, "These young men, although they took my son's life in the manner they did, we need to fight for them. Because they are going to come back out, and they will be older. But if they have no light, then this same disease is going to repeat itself, and they are going to take another person's child's life and eventually their own. And every mother's heart must feel this. We have to fight for them to see that there is a better life."

Through reframing, she verbalized her understanding of the unfortunate cycle that is bound to continue should factors that create criminality (such as environment, lack of resources, a dearth of support systems, education and negative mental programs of modern music) are allowed to persist.

She was able to forgive because simply put, she removed herself from her situation and emotions temporarily to see a case through the eyes of the perpetrator. She selflessly sought understanding by reframing her own experience and analyzing the factors that bring about crime in the first place, and found compassion and pity for murderers and optimism about the future, all of which allowed her to sacrifice her ego; an ego that would have damned them and as she demanded the death penalty. Compassion and sacrifice pushed her to want help change the course of the future so that she could ensure the survival of another mother's child. She tried to offset the potential another person would die at the hands of these perpetrators if she didn't seek to heal their dysfunction through love.

The steps leading to forgiveness are easy. The most challenging part is managing the emotions that you consciously or subconsciously harbor. If more people understood that strength is not what you hold on to but what you let go, there would be less aggression, less anger, and animosity; all of which encourages outrage that inevitably leads to violence and discord on some level, whether great or small. Many people find it very difficult to release negative emotions because of personal reasons.

This is indeed what makes people unforgiving.

Unfortunately, the odds chance that anyone could love everybody and everything is remote and are hindered because the ego will always stand in the way of understanding. It will also prevent emotion from prompting compassion for everyone and everything, and it will stop any effort to sacrifice something for everyone and everything. Without these elements, there will never be a willingness to give one's own life for everyone or everything.

Always know, some people will perpetually want to be angry and miserable. Love is made up of many things that fall under the purview of love. To love, you must first have the desire to do so. With all the woes in the world today, imagine, if everyone understood this concept; how race relations would improve.

Printed in Dunstable, United Kingdom

64290267R00119